COMMON SENSE:

DO NOT PLAY THE GAME WITH AN INMATE !!!

By
CC FANN

JABS Publications LLC
Wrightsville, Ga.

Contact Information:

C C Fann

JABS Publications LLC
P O Box 81
Wrightsville, GA 31096
478-278-7956

Email address

Jabspub@yahoo.com
OR
Ccfann@ccfanncommonsense.com

PRISON RAPE ELIMINATION ACT SIGNED BY PRESIDENT BUSH- SEPTEMBER 4, 2003 PUBLIC LAW 108-79 PROVIDES FOR THE ANALYSIS OF THE INCIDENT AND EFFECTS OF PRISONER SEXUAL ABUSE (RAPE). PROMOTES THE ERADICATION AND ELIMINATION OF RAPE WITHIN CORRECTIONS. PROTECTS SOCIETY AT LARGE.

PRISONER-ON- PRISONER SEXUAL ASSAULT & VICTIMIZATION STAFF-ON-PRISONER, SEXUAL MISCONDUCT & SEXUAL HARASSMENT

APPLIES NATIONALLY TO: ALL FEDERAL, STATE, AND LOCAL INSTITUTIONS PRISONS, JAIL, AND COMMUNITY CORRECTIONS PUBLIC AND PRIVATE JUVENILE AND ADULT

MALE AND FEMALE

STAFF-ON-PRISONER, STAFF-ON-INMATE, OR STAFF-ON-OFFENDER:
Prisoners are never regarded as being in a position to grant legitimate consent.

In Loving Memory

Of

Leman "Rooster" Fann and Louise "Doll" Fann

My grandparents

I miss you

FOREWORD

A good friend of mine, who is also a fellow co-worker, asked me to write about staff that fall in love with inmates or even write about why staff members have personal dealings with inmates. As we stood in his office window, we watched the CERT team escort an inmate from the isolation-segregation unit. He had been in the unit for two months for pending investigations. The inmate had a relationship with a female staff member. He was escorted to the Warden's office to meet with the Warden, Deputy Warden of Security and Captain.

The punishment that awaited him would pale in comparison to the fate awaiting the consenting female officer.

No, I never had personal dealings with an inmate but it has affected me as an employee, friend, co-worker and family member. All of us who are dedicated to the mission of the Department of Corrections often debate why anyone would give up their livelihood, respect, and health to have a relationship with an inmate.

What you are about to read is a book that will enhance and educate anyone who wishes to be employed with the Department of Corrections.
It will also further train employees as well.

So, in the next ten chapters, I plan to give you a synopsis of what the question, answer and solution is to why there is personal dealing in the prison, state institution, jails and youth development campuses. Why do staff members turn to inmates for love, friendship, and business dealings?

Introduction

ENTERING THE GATE
THE FIRST TIME

Before you became an officer or employee of the Department of Corrections, you were informed that you needed to take a test and make a certain score in order to be hired. You filled out the application. On the application was one question that made the most difference:

Have you committed a felony or misdemeanor? If so, list them.

By now, you should have figured out that you could not get a job with the Department of Corrections and break the law. Better yet, you could not associate with anyone who had broken the law.

Next, you get the call for an interview. You get dressed, travel to the interview, and are asked to fill out more paperwork, including the application. Then you are asked to sit in a lobby with other people who are interviewing for the same job. They call your name, and you are escorted by one of the interviewers, who tells you not to be nervous. You walk in and are asked to introduced yourself and have a seat. It's just like any other interview: you do not know the people on the interview board. You just know they are important.

Now the questions begin. Some pertain to supervising inmates. The questions usually go as follows: *What are your supervising skills? If an inmate cursed you, what would you do? If an inmate asked you to bring him something, what would you do?* Again, they are telling you that you cannot have personal dealings with inmates.

You go home, and you hope, pray, and worry about getting the job. For obvious reasons, you either need or want a job with the Department of Corrections. Everyone knows that the state has great benefits and now that the salary has been upgraded to $24,500 a year, the starting pay is good.

You finally get the call—you got the job! Now there is more paperwork to be done. You are asked to get a physical, which you will have to pay for. When they inform you that the background check through National Crime Information Center (NCIC) is complete, you are now clear to work for the Department of Corrections.

Already you have entered the institution twice, and each time you are asked at the front entrance, *Do you have any drugs, weapons, cell phones, chewing gum, or anything that will assist with the escape of an inmate?*

When you enter the lobby, you are questioned again. At this time, you have to enter a metal detector. You must empty your pockets, place everything in a tray, and walk through the metal detector. Some institutions require you to take off your shoes.

Once you have cleared the metal detector and gathered up the belongings you are allowed to keep (you must carry any ineligible items back to your car), then you can enter the facility. You are informed that you will be checked this way every time you enter the institution. This is the policy, which states, *Once you enter state property, you can be searched at any time.*

After everything has been completed, they give you your start date. Your required attire is black pants and a white button-down shirt, but nothing tight nor revealing. You need to report on the first or sixteenth of the month at 0715 hours.

On your first day of duty, you report to the briefing room and meet your first supervisor. Yes, you go through the same drill again to enter the institution. At this time, your appointed supervisor gives you an overview of the department. You are given an explanation of the requirements of your employment and are placed with a field-training officer. Your supervisor provides you with your working schedule and instructions on how to report any occurrences. Your supervisor also alerts you to the three-day training you will need to attend before going to the four-week training.

You are placed with veteran officers, usually field training officers. You will be observing offenders for the first time. Some offenders will address you just to get your reaction and evaluate you as an officer, whether you will make it or not. They look at how you walk, talk, make eye contact, respond to inmates' remarks. They observe how you observe your surroundings. By now, offenders have already begun to label you as a good or bad officer. Some institutions allow you, as a part of your training, to come in on Saturday and Sunday to observe visitation. They may even allow you to work rotating shifts so that you can familiarize yourself with inmates on different shifts before going off to Basic Correctional Officer Training.

Basic Correctional Officer Training is a four-week program that the state has set up to better prepare new correctional officers to supervise offenders. In this four-week course, new officers take classes like Interpersonal Communication Skills, CPR and First Aid, Fire and Safety, and Sexual Harassment. New officers are also instructed on how to shoot a .38 caliber gun and a 12 gauge shotgun, and they have to pass a firing range test.

During this week, you are away from your family and friends except on weekends. You also have a nightly curfew. You have to report every morning at 0745 hours, and each week you are tested on the information given during the week. You have to pass tests each week to keep your job; if you fail, you can be sent home. If you fail, it is up to the institution to decide whether or not you remain employed. The institution can give you a second chance and resend you through the training. If you're allowed to return to training, you may continue to earn a check.

With all that regimentation, you might think you had enlisted in the military, but remember this: nowhere in class did anyone tell you to sleep with inmates or bring them drugs, home-cooked meals, guns or knives, CDs, or anything else an inmate cannot have.

Why, I ask you, *go through all that training and give it up for an inmate?*

During this training, you are informed that your primary duty is to protect the public, protect the inmates, and provide a secure environment. While you are employed by the Department of Corrections, the administration is constantly encouraging you and giving you the opportunity to go back to school and further your education.

The Department of Corrections makes it totally clear that they are against any personal dealings with inmates. They have videos that show the consequences of violating this rule. Violations result in a charge of a felony and possibility of becoming one of the inmates that you were there to supervise. The department informs you that inmates are state property, and if you do anything with or toward them, you will be charged and/or terminated. You sign acknowledgement forms stating you have seen the video and know the rules and regulations on this policy.

After this strenuous four-week program, you graduate with pride. Now you can finally wear your blue uniform and your badge.

Once you report back to the institution, you are given your tour of duty, which is the shift you are assigned to and the time you need to report. Beginners are usually assigned to the second shift; they report at 1345 hours. In your briefing, you are given a post assignment, usually a dorm that houses 90 to 96 inmates. The last thing your supervisors say is, "Know your Basics and Beyond, which are key control, tool control, inmate accountability, sanitation, training, visibility of higher staff, programs, policies and procedures, fairness, consistency, honesty, zero tolerance for sexual and unlawful harassment, and personal dealings are against the rules and regulations."

Why would you go through all of that and give it up for an inmate?

CHAPTER 1

SETTING:
ORGANIZATION AND STRUCTURE

Before I begin this chapter, here are three main points to remember.

The first point is that each Department of Corrections has a mission and duties. As in any organization, you must know what your department stands for. If you carry out this mission, along with the Basics and Beyond, you will have a long-term career in corrections.

The next point is the chain of command. As a correctional officer, your chain of command is as follows (moving up from your rank): Correctional Officer and/or Correctional Officer II, Sergeant, Lieutenant, Captain or Chief of Security, Deputy Warden of Security, Warden, Field Operations Manager, Division Director, Assistant Facilities

Director, Facilities Director, Commissioner and the governor of the state. The Department of Corrections has a sound structure for an organization. It will often be repeated that you need to use for chain of command unless you have a problem with your immediate supervisor. This is when you can go up to the next level.

The third point is that the department has given you a resource that you can use when dealing with on the job situations or personal issues that may affect your job. That resource is the Employee Assistance Program. As a beginning correctional officer and/or non-security staff member, you have resources that you can use to do your job effectively. You are not alone when dealing with inmates. Using your chain of command or the Employee Assistance Program can save your job.

Now that you are a trained professional, you are about to enter a different world, a world that belongs to the inmates.

The old saying that an "inmate has nothing but time" is as real as it gets. You will work eight hours and fifteen minutes a day as an officer. An inmate is an inmate twenty-four hours a day, seven days a week, and (depending on his sentence) 365 days to life without parole.

What that means is you have different kinds of inmates:

1. Inmates that just want to do their time
2. Inmates that are snitches
3. Inmates that are in denial, refusing to admit that they are inmates. These latter inmates usually have no respect for authority and fall under the category of gang-bangers and thugs.
4. Officer-friendly inmates who often volunteer to assist and do work details
5. Inmates with mental illness and mental retardation.

When you report to your post, you are assigned to a housing unit with a maximum of 96 inmates. All five types of inmates are housed there. As long as you are an officer, you will be in their version of *the inmate game*. You may not know it yet, but you have been drafted in their game to play against them.

As in any job, you have resources; you have to implement teamwork and have common sense. In other words, when in doubt, ask someone who knows. Why go through all of this and give up your career for an inmate?

CHAPTER 2

SUPERVISION OF INMATES:
ALL EYES ARE ON YOU

As we continue, I will often refer to the Basic Correction Officer Training. This is where the supervision of different kinds of inmates is discussed in detail.

As a human being a saying that comes to mind is, "Treat people the way you want to be treated," or, as it says in Matthew 7:12, "Therefore all things whatsoever ye would that men should do to you, do ye even so to them."

The Department of Corrections has given us rules and regulations to use in supervising inmates. Throughout the years, jails and other corrections institutions have been under scrutiny for all the bad things that have happened there, like instances of racism, overcrowding, lack of food, religious differences, and abuse toward inmates.

The department states that you need to be fair and consistent when dealing with inmates. You will speak to inmates in a tone of respect, and you will not use profanity. You cannot deny inmates food, medical attention, or religious preferences. Inmates will receive counseling. Sanitation has to be 100 percent every day. You also have to protect inmates from other inmates. What more, you may ask, can the Departments give an inmate? Inmates already know that you cannot let them out early or release them unless you assist in helping them escape. If you do that, you will become an inmate yourself due to rule violation. The decision to release any inmate before the max-out date is up to the Board of Pardon and Paroles.

As stated earlier, one type of inmate refuses to admit that he is in prison. This inmate wants to live as if he were still on the streets. He does not like the rules that tell him he has certain times to be locked down, when lights-out and lights-on are, when and where to eat, when his clothes need to be washed, when he can get a haircut or shave. Yes, there is always someone in his face giving him instructions. He does not like it that he has to be ready for inspection. *He just does not like the rules.* Although he may play by the rules, he does not like them, and given the opportunity, he will break the rules.

This inmate will say to you, "You can wear this outfit, just like me." He says this to make you feel guilty that he is locked up. He often says, "I'm a grown-ass man and you cannot tell me what to do." He will make that statement until he wants something from you.

The second type of inmate is the wise guy. He wants the other inmates to respect him. But since he cannot rule other inmates with brute force, the wise guy has to come up with an edge. An edge can be as simple as working on the kitchen detail and providing extra servings for their fellow inmates, at a price, or working in the laundry, washing clothes in the special wash. Special wash laundry does not contain concentrated detergent or state detergent.

The wise guy always has a hustle. Once he establishes himself as a businessman, he makes his move. He searches for his target, a correctional officer who will fall for his hustle.

The inmate that is a snitch sits and watches everything. He has different ways to inform management of what he sees. He may write a letter to the captain (or someone further up the chain of command) to let them know what is going on inside the prison. Some snitches will send false information up the chain of command just to get officers and other inmates in trouble. All snitches know that any information that goes to upper management will be acknowledged and/or investigated.

Officer-friendly inmates are the ones that often volunteers for work details. They like to stay busy to make their time go by a little faster. They hate being on the housing unit, so you will find them volunteering for details like buffing and waxing the floors or doing sidewalk details by picking up trash. The officer friendly inmate does not want to get involved in compromising situations. He is the inmate who is involved with the majority of personal dealings with the staff. This inmate becomes very familiar with the staff by doing things for staff members even when asked not to. He thus gets himself into a position where he is unnoticed, but he can always hear what the staff is discussion. He can tell you when someone has gotten demoted, terminated, or moved to another shift. He knows when the wardens are being rotated and for what reason. He knows who is sleeping with whom. This inmate belongs to a national syndicated newspaper that I like to call the CNN. This is the Convict National Newspaper.

It's true: all these eyes will be on you as you continue to work for the Department of Corrections.

CHAPTER 3

SELLING DREAMS
AND MAKING FALSE PROMISES
Mathol Jordan

Now we come to the topic I have been waiting to share with you. Sometimes officers allow inmates to play staff.

The following are scenarios that have led to firing of correctional officers:

1. A female food service supervisor is investigated for having a sexual relationship with an inmate on her detail.
2. A work detail officer goes out to lunch and brings back a meal for her inmate.
3. A sergeant falls in love with an inmate on her work detail. Every time she is moved to another shift, she has the officer to sign the inmate out so they can be together for long periods of time ... as if he were still on a work detail.

4. An officer leaves a piece of candy in plain view for her dorm orderly to pick it up as trash.

5. An officer interested in gambling asks an inmate what the weekly favorite picks are.

6. Male and female officers bring cell phones into the prison for a sum of money. The cell phone as registered in their names.

7. A female staff member puts in a request to work a certain post to be near an inmate. Whether it is raining or not, she wears a raincoat to hide the hole in her pants between her legs. This hole allows easy access for the inmate to have sex with her in the utility closet.

8. A staff member catches a female prison industry worker giving oral sex to a male inmate.

9. A worker allows an inmate's family members to stay with her on the weekend so they can visit with their inmate. The family pays the worker.

10. A staff member holds a conversation with another staff member, discussing a fellow employee in front of inmates.

11. An outside detail officer allows his inmates to have conjugal visits with their significant others while on the work detail.

12. A back gate officer neglects to search an inmate, knowing that the inmate has drugs on him.

How does all of this happen? you may ask. My answer comes from Mathol Jordan, a good friend and superior staff member: *Inmates are selling dreams and making false promises.*

At some point in time, we have relationships in our personal lives that become tormented. We have breakups and/or divorces. We are not appreciated at home or on the job. Sometime staff members become disgruntled, and perhaps we feel that our supervisors are showing favoritism. We take financial blows that put us in difficult situations. You may have family members who are incarcerated. They have run-ins with the law, and you come to feel sorry for inmates in general, but these are not excuses to become involved with an inmate.

This is where inmates become predators. They prey on you just like a lion in the jungle stalks an antelope. They watch and wait for their prey to wander away from the herd so they can attack. Inmates sell you dreams that you think you can rely on. They tell you that you are the greatest officer they ever saw. They give you inside info about upper management, they alert you when supervisors are making their rounds, they pass along gossip they have overheard. They offer you large sums of money to bring items in to them, such as drugs, cell phones, and porno magazines.

The ultimate dream is when an inmate says something like, "No one will know but you and me." Or, "I am not like the rest, because I am a real convict." Or, "I got you."

But these are dreams and false promises. There are no excuses to become involved with an inmate.

CHAPTER 4

WHAT ARE THEY TELLING YOU
THAT MAKES YOU FALL IN LOVE WITH THEM?

A Deputy Warden once asked me, "Fann, all I want to know is what are these inmates telling staff members to make them want to participate in a relationship with them?" I also remember the words of a former warden, who said, "Don't get your money where you get your honey." When I first heard that, it was funny. Later on, I heard that a female officer was fired for having a sexual relationship with a female inmate.

I often find that being attractive is a good thing, but in the world that prison inmates inhabit, it does not matter how you look. Inmates are men and women first, but members of the prison staff need to remember one crucial fact: we are doing a job. We were not hired to fulfill the sexual needs of the inmates. Just because they tell you that you look nice, your perfume smells good, or you smell nice, that does not mean you should pay attention and succumb to them. An inmate might say, "I like way you wear your hair. You need to tell your coworkers to go where you get your hair done." He might use this same flattering approach and ask you if you have you been working out or if he can do anything for you. He always asks with a smile.

Inmates love to be engaged in long conversations on sports, too, and they may even use the Bible and discuss religion just to get your attention.

The inmates are trying to get you to see them without their prison uniform on, to see them as good guys and not prison inmates. Let me elaborate: the inmate wants you to respect him. He wants you to forget he is incarcerated.

Yes, there are attractive inmates, men who have made mistakes. But common sense should tell us three things:

1. You are employed to do a job. You are not employed to have a personal relationship with an inmate.

2. Your self-esteem should not be so low that you take the word of an inmate as truth.

3. You should not sacrifice your self respect or the respect of your family, friends, and coworkers to have a relationship with an inmate. Why give up all the hard work you went through for an inmate?

Erring staff members are often escorted out through the same gates they entered seeking employment. Staff members need to remind themselves that they do not need an inmate's words, not their flattery and compliments, not their money, and especially not their sexual attraction and consummation.

Case No. 111

A female officer was having a sexual relationship with an inmate from Atlanta, Georgia, whose rival gang members in the dorm were from Savannah. She was bringing drugs, paraphernalia, and porn movies and magazines in for this inmate, and she and the

inmate were having sex in the cell while another inmate acted as lookout. During chow one day, an inmate from Savannah began talking about how this officer was a whore. The inmate from Atlanta addressed him, and soon a fight broke out. There were two officers in the dining area with 70 to 80 inmates. The officers were not only greatly outmanned but severely injured while trying to break up this altercation. Later, when a rival gang member reported what the officer was doing, she was investigated and charged. Her husband divorced her and took custody of their two children. She was charged by the state and did time in the state prison for women.

Inmates are being physically assaulted and rape by each other every day. With HIV and AIDS on the rise in the inmate population, no sexual encounter is safe.

But remember—these inmates, both men and women, have been or will be locked up for a long time. They will not be with intimate with the opposite sex for a long time. Even unattractive characters on

TV shows, like Esther and Fred on *Sanford and Son*, Archie Bunker on *All in the Family*, and JJ on *Good Times*, will look good to them!

Here's the bottom line. If you take this same inmate and set him free, and you see him walking in the mall, and you, the same officer, walk past him, he probably will not speak or acknowledge you. It is only while he is locked up that he wants to give you all his attention.

CHAPTER 5

THE PART TIME JOB:
BUSINESS DEALINGS WITH INMATES

As I stated earlier, sometime in their life everyone falls on financially hard times. Some people are greedy and live beyond their means. Some are naive and truly believe they will never get caught being financially stupid or dishonest. They think no one will ever see what they do. Other people are hustlers and cannot stand to see a good deal go by. As a new employee, you might ask, *Why fool around and risk losing your job?* If you act dishonestly in the prison system, not only will you lose your job, but you may also be prosecuted for, say, bringing drugs in on government property. You can do ten to fifteen years in prison.

If you get a "part-time job" (working for an inmate), it is plainly and simply for money. You are an employee or staff member. If you bring in contraband to an inmate, you become a mule. In western movies, you will see the cowboy riding his horse leading several mules harnessed to a rope. These mules are used to carry heavy items or items the cowboy does not want in his possession. He may not want to weigh down his horse. If the cowboy decides to get rid of dead weight, he may cut a mule loose. You are carrying things an inmate does not want in his possession. Cutting you loose like a mule is what the inmate will do to you when he turns you in.

While you are thinking the inmates love and appreciate you as an officer because you are doing them a favor, you are actually only a mule in their eyes. There have been plenty mules before you, and it saddens me to say there will be more mules after you leave.

Contraband is any item that the state does not issue to an inmate. Contraband items include guns, knives, drugs, alcohol, cell phones, and porno magazines. These are things that mules carry. Yes, employees have brought weapons to inmates.

This is where you come in.; they have to manipulate you to bring the items in for them. They do not care how you bring the contraband in as long as you deliver. They do not even care that you may get caught and be embarrassed by your peers.

You may bring a contraband item in taped to your leg, in your lunch bag, hidden in a dinner plate, made up in a sandwich. Women may use sanitary items (tampons and pads) to hide contraband items. You may simply just put it in your pocket.

Now, after you have brought in the contraband, how will you get paid? Some inmates will have family members who will mail you money in the form of cash, a check, or a money order. Some inmates receive cash smuggled in through visitation, and they give you cash on the spot. Inmates do not care how you are paid as long as you deliver.

It is when you do not deliver, when you hesitate to be a mule again, or do not want to take certain customers that your part-time job starts to be evaluated. Remember that you cannot satisfy all the inmates.

Question: *Do you think an inmate is going to finance you when you get caught?* Do you think he will pay your bills? Do you think he will hire a lawyer for you if you are charged? Why would you even think he would help you when he could not help? How can he help you when he could not stop himself from being locked up?

That is why these two words are important. COMMON SENSE. You have to use common sense. If you have participated in any illegal business prior to your employment, you already have knowledge of the risks. You do not care if you are caught. But if you never broke any laws and obtain a job in law enforcement, why would you take a part-time job and risk finding your photo on the front page of the local newspaper?

CC Fann

Newspapers constantly highlight law enforcement employees who break the law. They say we should know better. We are supposed to be role models and set the standard. We wear a badge like Matt Dillon in *Gunsmoke*. Newspaper writers are correct. As public employees, we are highly respected by the community. We need to always keep that in mind.

CHAPTER 6

CONFESS OR KEEP PLAYING THE GAME?

If you are playing the game of personal dealings with inmates, it is like you are asleep. You are apparently out cold, unaware of the real world. You are like Sleeping Beauty waiting for Prince Charming to kiss and wake you up. You may be like Dorothy in the *Wizard OZ* asking yourself "There is no place like home". If you are playing the game with inmates, you must have been asleep during your training. Your job, your health, and the well being of your family will be taken away from you. Your fellow workers will cease to respect you. The oath you took as a correctional officer or employee of the state will go out the window when you have personal dealings with an inmate. Then you wake up wondering how long it will be until the investigative staff questions you about your actions.

There is no one you can trust. In the policy, all staff members who know about any personal dealings are required to report what they know. Failure to report personal dealing can result in disciplinary actions with the maximum being termination. For example, at a female facility, two good friends worked in housing units side by side, Buildings F-1 and F-2, on a six-day rotation. The housing units held female offenders guarded by female officers. Officer J was assigned to F-1, Officer M, to F-2. In F-2, Inmate Davis was a day orderly whose job was cleaning, all day, every day, and she even volunteered to clean the sidewalk and windows in front of the dorm. When smoke break was called, she reported out. Inmate Davis always went out first and went next door to talk to Officer J.

The rest of the inmates recognized her behavior and claimed that Officer J was showing favoritism toward Inmate Davis. The inmates stated to Officer M that Inmate Davis was making phone calls to Officer J at her residence. Every time Officer M worked in F-2, the inmates constantly made statements to her about Inmate Davis's behavior, which Officer M recognized. Not knowing that the inmates had already sent written statements to administration that there were personal dealings between Officer J and Inmate Davis, Officer M failed to report this behavior and the statements the inmates were making to her supervisor.

When the investigation started, Officer M stated that she did not want to get involved. Then it was found that Officer J was having a sexual relationship with Inmate Davis. Letters were found in the inmate's cell. The phone calls that the inmate was making were going to Officer J's mother's residence. Those phone calls were being recorded by the prison. In the end, Officer J confessed to personal dealings with Inmate Davis. She was terminated. But Officer M was also penalized. She received written a reprimand and was given a five percent reduction in pay for a year for her failure to report personal dealings.

Yes, you must report personal dealings.

If you are engaged in personal dealings with an inmate, this example may make you feel nervous and paranoid. You may begin wondering who is watching you. You may start asking yourself if your supervisor or fellow officers know what you have been doing. In training, all staff members are informed that they are required to report personal dealings.

Are the inmates talking? Every time your supervisor calls, your blood pressure will go up. No matter how many excuses you make to the inmate that you cannot do what he or she asks, you know you cannot get out of this situation. You know the inmate will not take no for an answer. You begin to feel threatened and pressured. You need to understand that this would never happen if you lived by the policy, if you said no to the inmate and reported the inmate.

When you work in a prison, you are an inmate...except that you have a correctional officer's uniform on. You know you will eventually pay the consequences for your wrong-doings. You will feel that you need to be placed in a cell. You can only hope the inmate will get shipped out or released.

CHAPTER 7

INVESTIGATIONS:
The kites have flown up north.

The word "kite" is defined as a light framework covered with cloth, plastic, or paper. It is designed to climb and fly in a steady breeze at the end of a long string.

In the inmate game in prison, a kite is an informant, a snitch. The kite is the person who informs the administration about what is going on in the prison. Just like a kite, a snitch will inform on someone by writing on a piece of cloth, plastic, or paper. But instead of flying in a breeze, this kind of kite travels in other ways. It can be passed from hand to hand, come or go in institutional or regular mail, be delivered by a family member, or be delivered in a conversation with a staff member.

This kind of kite can be very dangerous. When the message has been delivered, if nothing else, it can cast a shadow of doubt over an officer. Such a doubt usually cannot be erased, dismissed, or forgotten, for once the kite arrives at its destination, it sets off a chain reaction. The kite will name people (staff members), places, dates, and times and. All these details will be investigated.

Let us use Officer Bob as our example. Bob is assigned to the third shift. The kite states that on Friday, April 8, Officer Bob is scheduled to pick up a drop of $50 to buy ten $5 bags of marijuana for Inmate Bernard, who will give him the money on Friday. Bernard is the middleman. He has been intimidated by other inmates to become a deliveryman. But Bernard is tired of being in the middle. He is afraid of doing more time. He becomes a kite. The middleman writes a letter to prison administration.

Now the investigation begins. Administrators question the inmate. Usually, the inmate will save himself and sell the officer out by suggesting a set-up.

The officer will receive marked bills. These transactions always work in cash because a money order can be traced. It is easy to learn who bought it and who cashed it.

The inmate now waits patiently and soon makes the arrangements with Officer Bob. After the transaction is complete, and Officer Bob has committed his crime, the supervisor comes to Bob's dorm and gets the signal from the inmate that Bob has the money. Officer Bob is unexpectedly relieved early that day, and as he is signing out, some officers are picked "randomly" to be searched. Officer Bob is of course one of them. The marked bills are found in his pocket.

Officer Bob is now questioned. They show him a photocopy of the money to show that it was marked on purpose. He is advised to write a statement. In his statement, he may say that he found the money on the sidewalk. According to departmental policy, when you find something, including contraband items, on state grounds, you need to report this to your supervisor immediately and fill out an incident report, a chain of custody report, and a witness statement.

Officer Bob does not, of course, admit that he got the money from Inmate Bernard. At this time, the investigation goes to another level, Internal Affairs. While this is going on, Bob faces three options: (1) he may be placed on administrative leave with pay, (2) he may be placed on administrative leave without pay, or (3) he may be suspended without pay. While Bob waits for the official investigation, more kites are flying. He will probably get blamed for the misdeeds of other dirty officers and become a scapegoat.

Let us do the math. After Bob brings in the drugs, he makes about $50 profit. At the same time, Bob loses his estimated gross salary of $26,000. If he is charged, he needs to retain a lawyer at the minimum of $500. If Bob is convicted, he loses not only his income, but also his self-respect, dignity, and the capacity to work with the Department of Corrections. All for only $50.

See? Kites are very important in the prison system. Sometimes they inform you of riots and disturbances that may be about to happen. More important, they help administration to weed out officers who will be at jeopardy at the institution, those who that may be doing personal dealings. Why would administration wait to catch the drugs on the officer or the inmate?

1. Most of the time, they will wait until the crime actually takes place, but if the kite is wrong, there is a liability issue.

2. Administration does not know if or when the officer will ever bring the drugs in again.

3. The kite is an inmate. He may be lying.

4. The department can wait until the officer brings the drugs in, and then bring in the canine unit to check the area for drugs. Inmates can also be tested for drugs.

Inmates that test positive are placed in segregation for pending investigation. Then more kites start flying. The captain completes the paperwork and forwards it to the Internal Affairs. The officer being investigated may be asked to take a lie detector test.

What if you are Officer Bob? For $50, you lose everything.

What if you passed all these tests? You are cleared, the kite is shipped to another prison, and you are now inherited by another inmate to continue doing business.

CHAPTER 8

CLEAN ADDRESS

John Ford

Officers, especially female officers, are nothing but a clean address to inmates.

This kind of inmate is a two-time loser or a gang banger who has destroyed family ties. A two-time loser is in prison for the second time and cannot parole back to his previous residence or address. He has a parole date. His primary mission is to get a clean address. Meaning? A place where no one knows him? The gang banger has cut off his ties from his family. He will not jeopardize his immediate family's health or well being or does not want his family to be a liability. He looks for female officers who like thugs or club goers.

Inmates do not care what the female officer looks like. It doesn't matter if she is pretty or ugly, short or tall, fat or thin, as long as she is a law-abiding citizen with a clean address an address that's not in jail? He is set on finding her weakness so he can break her down, and he does not care how long it takes. Once he has control, he will not allow her to bring in drugs or any contraband. There will be no sex. He will simply keep feeding her ego. He will keep her clean in administration's eyes

This officer is usually a good and outstanding officer, and so when the allegations come out, no one believes she is having personal dealings with the inmate. The officer knows the inmate's plan, but for it to be successful the officer will retire, resign, or transfer. Usually the officer will say she is going back to school or looking for another job.

The inmate transfer to another prison to keep the heat off both of them.

To sum up, the inmate's mission is to set up a law abiding citizen to parole or max out to. He will not live in your world. He loves fast money and is a career criminal. You will have to play in his version of *Bonnie and Clyde*. Yes, the inmate says you are the one for him. He wants to spend his life with you. Maybe he says he has a hidden stash that will take care of both of you. "You don't need this low paying job," he purrs. "I can take care of all your bills."

Common sense should remind you that you are already taking care of your bills. How do you know he really has a stash? What about the man or woman this inmate left behind that may have stood by him? When the inmate enters prison, is he going to turn his back on the ones who have been sending him money? And what will your family think of you for bringing an ex-con home around your children, if you have any?

If a man and woman in the free world begin to date, they usually check each other out. If need be, you will call the FBI to check him out. You will investigate what kind of job he has, who his family is, how much money he or she makes, and how many kids he has.

An inmate does not get paid in prison. He has no retirement plan. He has no health benefits. The only thing he is guaranteed is a $25 release check and a bus ticket. Are you willing to check and see how many crimes your inmate has committed? Have you ever read any of your inmate's court transcripts?

Society is changing, but not fast enough. When a man is released from prison, it is hard for him to get a good job. All jobs and apartment managers are doing background checks now. His past crimes will hold him back.

Common sense and your training will tell you that he cannot parole out home for one or more of the following reasons:

1. He may have a drug charge. With a drug charge, he cannot live in any federal funded apartments (including Section 8 or urban projects). He may have lived there with his girlfriends in the past, but he can't go back.
2. With a child molestation charge, he may be forbidden to live where he used to live, especially if his old residence is near a school. Part of his parole or probation states that he cannot reside near a school..
3. Someone in the household has previous charges.

4.   He owes the mob or mafia.

5.   He may have turned state's evidence.

6.   He has hurt his family so deeply that they have turned their backs on him.

7.   He has given his significant other HIV/AIDS.

Do any of these reasons make you say *Hmmmm?*

Do not accept the usual excuses people make, like "Everyone makes mistakes," or "A small mistake is the same as a big mistake." Do not accept these excuses for being caught up in an inmate game. Common sense will tell you never to make any mistakes on purpose.

A clean address is what you will have for an inmate or probationer when he is released. His probation and/or parole officer will check out his residence before he is released. They will stipulate that he cannot be released back to his old neighborhood because of the high crime rate. He will be a high risk to return to prison.

Your residence will be a place for him to get back on his feet. All the bills are already in your name, and you (of course) will be the one paying them. You will have groceries and a hot shower. You will have a car so he can get around. You will give him all the sex he wants and needs, and you will want to please him. He will use you until he gets off parole or probation. Once he has no use for you, however, he will go back home and to his former girlfriend.

The reason this plan does not work with a high percentage Is the he officer allows her emotions to take over. She wants more contact and writes letters for him. She will take risks by passing his letters and using the institutional mail. She may even bring in a cell phone so she can talk to him every day.

And she will get caught if she does not resign first. The snitch will begin to send kites to administrators and the mailroom. Every institution is thorough when it searches the incoming and outgoing mail, so your letters will be caught.

You will also be violating another policy: you cannot have any personal dealing with a parolee or probationer and even a family member unless it is approved through your administration. You must report all personal dealings.

For example, let's say a correctional officer resigns. Two months later, this ex-correctional officer and her boyfriend are stopped on the interstate for drug trafficking. In their possession are thirty pounds of cocaine and $13,000 in cash. After the investigation, it is discovered that the ex-officer's boyfriend was an inmate at the prison where the officer was previously employed.

If you fall for the clean address game, four things are likely to happen. You will become an addict. You will go to jail. You will go broke. You will be abandoned as soon as your usefulness is over.

CHAPTER 9

RESIGNATION OR TERMINATION

The question is "To be are not to be?" You have been played. You cannot trust anyone. You hate coming to work. Now you are in a maze thinking there is no way out. You keep asking yourself these three questions:

1. Do I resign?
2. Do I wait and hear the outcome of the investigation?
3. Do I attempt to transfer to another prison with a valid excuse?

If you resign, they may ask you, "Did you really do it?" There may be a chance that you could be hired again by the state, but remember that, like the inmates, the staff will talk. The chance that you will be rehired after you resign is a slim one. Rumors, gossip, and lies will keep circulating around you. You will be in an uncomfortable position.

So your reputation as an officer has been damaged beyond repair. What do you do?

Let me tell you, if there is any time to open your mouth, now is that time. Whether you believe it or not, *there is somebody you can trust.*

If you find yourself in a compromising position, you have your chain of command to rely on. Most wardens and superintendents have an open-door policy. You can go to this supervisor and disclose things in confidence. There is a possibility that after you talk with them they may use you to set the inmate up. It is never too late. Do not feel that you are alone.

The Department of Corrections trains and retrains employees every year to keep them up to date on policies. One of the tasks your supervisors have is to make sure you are doing your job efficiently. If you look bad, they look bad. They are there to help you. Do not fool yourself. Report what you have done, even if the infraction is relatively minor, like you fell asleep on the job and the inmate woke you up before the supervisor saw you. Play the inmate. Let him know you are not worried about him reporting you because you will report yourself. The same holds if you drop your keys and the inmate picks them up. An inmate knows he should not pick up keys. Let your supervisor know.

The blackmail or the leverage that the inmate has on you is nothing if you report it to your supervisor. If you resign or allow yourself to be terminated, the inmate has won. It is sad to say, but people always remember the bad things that happen.

If you are fired or terminated, this will definitely go down in the history books as a loss for the Department of Corrections.

CHAPTER 10

YOU DON'T HAVE TO LOSE

A beautiful female officer at a men's prison was having sex with an inmate. They had a lookout, another inmate. This other inmate waved to another officer on the unit to catch them right in the act. Not knowing what was happening, the officer approached the cell and witnessed the officer and the inmate having sexual intercourse. After the officer reported the incident to the shift officer in charge, the female officer was handcuffed and escorted out of the prison. She will be charged. If found guilty, she will serve ten years in a women's facility and be registered as a sex offender for the rest of her life. She will not be able to have sex with a man in the women's facility.

What is the lesson here? Stop the inmate before he puts you in a compromising position. Address anything he says to you by being professional. Tell him, "Keep any personal comments to yourself."

If an inmate is in your face for more than three minutes, this is carrying out a long conversation. He is attempting to get you hooked. If this goes on every day for three minutes or longer, you are hooked, though you may not know it. Believe me, the Convict National News has already written an article in the sports section declaring that you have lost the game.

The only discussion (unless you are a counselor, mental health professional, or chaplain) that a staff member needs to have for three minutes or longer is when he or she is investigating a situation. The only other time is when your supervisor instructs you to talk to an inmate.

Inmates only need to ask you about procedures regarding medical or counseling issues, religious issues, or about the commissary or their property. Once he begins a conversation on any other topic, you need to make an effort to refer him to the inmate handbook or to someone who is employed in those specialty departments. If his conversation is regarding security issues that an inmate may have questions about, document his concern and promptly notify your supervisor. It is not our business how much money an inmate has. We don't need to know when his significant other divorces or leaves him, if he never has visitations, or who his family is.

Also be aware of the small things, such as a simple bump between you and an inmate. This may imply something sexual or be an attempt to intimidate you. Do not engage in long eye contact or constantly discuss things in the free world with an inmate. Give him precise instructions and always leave your personal opinions and business outside the gate.

These are just a few things to keep in mind when dealing with inmates.

Most facilities house 1,200 to 1,700 inmates. You cannot have sex with all of them. You cannot bring in pounds of drugs to satisfy all of these addicts. You cannot even smuggle in any other paraphernalia. Why would you bring in a gun and knife that the inmate can easily use to kill you or a fellow staff member? You will get caught! Jealousy and envy on the part of other inmates who cannot get in on a good deal will surely get you fired. Keep this in mind: the inmate's own family members will not risk their freedom for him. Why should you?

Intercourse (both social and sexual) does not only happen in prisons. It is found in other departments, too, such as juvenile justice, county jails, probation detention centers, and transitional centers. All-female facilities also have this problem.

Paying attention to common sense, teamwork, and training will give you a long and outstanding career in corrections.

Report! Report! Report!

Question. Will you play the game and lose everything you have worked for an inmate?

CONCLUSION

DISCUSSION QUESTIONS

Take some time to consider and answer the following questions.

1. What are personal dealings?

2. Do you report personal dealing?

3. Do you bring anything to an inmate?

4. Do you discuss personal business with an inmate?

5. Do you use profanity toward an inmate?

6. Do you have sex with an inmate?

7. Do you have any personal dealings with an inmate's family?

8. When do you report personal dealings?

9. Who do you report personal dealings to?

10. Will you play inmate games?

CC Fann

A LETTER
FROM THE AUTHOR

I wrote this book to give advice on how to deal with inmates if you pursue a career with corrections. Because the best way to beat an inmate is become more knowledgeable than he is, I hope I said something that will help you. Having been a correctional officer for ten years, I have seen a lot and been through a lot. I believe that when bad things happen, it builds character so you will not do it again. I was sad to see good human beings walking out of our gates for doing the wrong thing.

The bad things I describe in this book should help build your character. They should strengthen you so you can grow and know what you are up against in this field. Believe me, inmates will take a new inmate under their wings and educate him or her on what to do and expect.

Staff members also take new staff under their wings. I felt it was necessary for me to do the same as others have done before me. I just want to help in the cause in leveling the playing field. I am a competitor and like to win. If I can save another staff member, I will.

When I wrote this book, it was to help new hires and anyone interested in becoming employed by the Department of Corrections. The simplicity and the manner of the writing are to give the basic facts about inmate games. If I repeated things more than once, I was making sure you got my point.

CC FANN
P.S. I hope you enjoy the book

ACKNOWLEDGMENTS

Thanks first to my Lord, Jesus Christ, the Father, and my savior, for allowing me to write this book and giving me the courage to step out in faith. You are first in my life.

Next, thanks to my children, Ashley, Anthony, Janique, and Janiah, for bringing joy to my life. I love you

Thanks to the Georgia Department of Corrections, especially Warden Anthony Washington; Warden Alexis E. L. Chaise, PhD; Unit Manager Mathol Jordan; and Warden John Ford. I thank them for giving me guidance and helping me succeed as a correctional officer. .

Thanks to my mother, Jant, to my sisters Tiff and Val, and to my brother, Chad. I may not say it often, but I do love you.

Thanks to my uncle, big brother, and father, Mr. Kenneth Williams, for the encouragement. You have served greatly in these roles.

Thanks to the Peanut Gallery—James Blair, Jerome Andrews, Tracey Poole, Neal Buley, Reginald Fordham, Donald Mckie, Tracey Poole, and Leticia Martin. It's been fun. Remember, you are on my VIP list.

Finally, thanks to Latasha Harrell, Crystal Baker, Courtney Thomas, Carolyn Liggins, Cynthia

Johnson, Anthony Reeves, Anita Hall and Mr. Sylvester Burton. Thank you for being my friends. Thanks to my church family for the support and encouraging words. Buckeye Baptist Church, East Dublin, GA

CC Fann

NOTES

_____

_____

_____

_____

_____

_____

_____

_____

_____

_____

_____

_____

_____

_____

_____

NOTES

_____

_____

_____

_____

_____

_____

_____

_____

_____

_____

_____

_____

_____

_____

NOTES

NOTES

CC Fann

Use this coupon to order via mail

Also available at
WWW.AMAZON.COM
WWW.CCFANNCOMMONSENSE.COM

Common Sense ☐ $15.00 ☐

Name_____

Address_____

City_____State_____Zi
p Code_____

Shipping and Handling $5

This offer subject to change without notice

Send checks or money orders to:

C C Fann

JABS Publications LLC
P O Box 81
Wrightsville, GA 31096
478-278-7956

Please allow 2-3 weeks for delivery.

For more information email: Jabspub@yahoo.com, or
Ccfann@ccfanncommonsense.com. You can also visit
www.ccfanncommonsense.com